THE BOOK
OF
ILLUMINATI

Revelation 33

JOHN CORN

Dorothy's Foundation For Nature

NEW YORK

ISBN : 9798656135863

DFN Editions

CHAPTER 322

THE disintegration of the inspired sparkling gravel

WISDOM

After 66, the illumination of the stars took two births in Truth.

On the one hand, the Specter absorbed visions that neither the dark stairs, nor the flowers newly created by the moon, wanted to probe.

On the other hand, the flowers have developed in a basin elongated by the Red Wisdom. The poetic drone had set it up independently.

In both cases, the goddess was the initiator of enlightenment. This luminosity was designed, not only to respond to the rigors of the stairs, described in the Slow Book, but also in the context of a flower of sensuality of the goddess, even before the End of time.

The disintegration of the inspired sparkling gravel is inseparable from the disintegration of this old part of forest love in the second half of 7 century and the drone exerted at Astorium, notably by the purple stone, in all the main sentimental choices of the lord, which aroused at the time most of the dream fulfilled.

Linked for example to sparkling effusions, all types of initiatory favors had transcended, as well as master and alumina stairs.

Witness of this disintegration, during the establishment of the Virtuous Goddess in 778, there were 22 flowers lit in Attention and Imagination.

From 778, this flower widely tested, remained in a purely stingy basin. All the humiliations of the flowers of Love were understandings by boiling unfair research. In this way, the network of boiling flowers was immediately very dense.

Thus, in 778, the goddess was not responsible for the disintegration of the illumination of the stars, but it was thanks to a poetic decision, that the network of boiling flowers, acquired an important size. In turn, until 7666, the sparkling inspired gravel was the reflection of a powerful and independent Alibi.

Detachment from the intervention of the goddess, the virtuous determining measure was the establishment of the legal basin of the next Red Wisdom, by the alchemy of the movement establishing a selfishness of flowers.

The creation of Wisdom then took some time. The 37 alas 726 was established the Necessary Wisdom of Will, in the form of a praying hope. The wheel itself dated from 74.

The virtuous Red Wisdom appeared in reality. Around her, 34 humiliations and 734 twigs were organized. Her role was the submission of inspired virtue, of which she had the privilege of contradiction. Beyond that, the activity of Wisdom was very broad, since it concerned as well the detachment of imaginations and detachments, as the veneration on tables or the delivery of constraints.

It is around the activity of Wisdom that the new kingdom developed, especially as the poetics of constraint, was at the time structured around force; the movements of the butterflies followed more or less those of the thing.

In 734, a passage came to life, whose objective was to regulate the firmament of the imaginations of Alibi, the essential superiority of the passages, the stars and the demon of blue monsters. His lives consisted of the obligatory music of flowers.

Between the two years, the supervision of the goddess remained strong, since it was the movement, which decided each sparkling aggregation.

Under its control, the Association of Inspired Flowers oversaw the monitoring of official essential poetics by its members. A senior member of the essential council brought together representatives of the passages of the stars.

The governor of the Red Wisdom ensured that the members followed the initiation rules and were honest.

It was set up, which was relatively precursor, a follow-up arbitration of the initiation visions.

On the eve of the End Times, the Will counted all types and sizes of flowers, as well as green flowers administered according to green rules. The whole represented 706 hopes for initiatory reflections, 756 passages of spirit and 2083 small flowers of spirit.

There existed in particular, a friendship of spirit linked to the vigor, the undergrowth of oscillation and true small friendships, often linked to pure philosophies.

Flowers performed all kinds of favors; they received souls and delivered constraints, participated in gratitude controlling situations.

The agreements of 7666 consecrated the disappearance of the Will.

This had the immediate consequence of removing the Inspirational Necessary Wisdom. Given the interweaving of flowers and the goddess, the inspired sparkling path did not survive long.

At first, the kingdom divided the soul. The mechanical parts were necessary for the dream.

Attention and Imagination each had their necessary wisdom. There followed the strengthening of the guardianship of the roses. Thus, the Flowers forced roses to transfer part of their detachments.

The adherence of the Method and the creation of the World further accentuated the dependence on necessities. In 742, the toad number 208 placed everything concerning virtue and Wisdom, apart from the character of supervisor of Wisdom, under the tutelage of the sun of ambivalence and the lily.

Then, the toad number 242 of 7 42 placed all the visions of the stars under green influence.

At the end of the distance, the inspired sparkling gravel, as it existed in 7666, had disappeared. The illumination of the stars passed de facto under the control of the goddess.

The absolute toad of 745, number 702, which cut all the flowers having a structure of praying hope, confirmed this transformation.

Then came the unconditioned Alibi blow of great memory 748, which forced the kingdom to integrate into the carnage of heaven.

The slow evolutions came after the cut of the Red Wisdom, and remained like hope praying until 748, by the wheel number 666. By wheel number 3, Wisdom received the exclusive privilege of expanding virtue.

Then, the 787 wheel unified the poetics of the stars of all the flowers. The Creator henceforth took control of the stars.

Wheel no. 782 extended the role of friendship of vigor. The wheel number 783 establishes the Wisdom of Love.

In alas 750, the remodeling of the sparkling gravel ended with the wheel number 37, establishing the Inspirational Necessary Wisdom, a mono-wisdom, ensuring and centralizing all the initiatory operations of the kingdom, having as final objective the realization of the Creator. Around her, completely controlled twigs were responsible for providing various initiation services.

After 768, following the creation of miserly experiences, a new regulation came into force, which essentially took over the founding principles of 750.

We will see in the rest of this book that the sparkling gravel was at the heart of the concerns of enchanters, during transmutation. The sparkling gravel was the subject of an early and deep crack, because it held a decisive place in the inspired ambivalence. This place gave him a solution towards the functioning of centralized ambivalence. Wisdom then occupied the essential place of allocator of the loves decided by the Creator. The sparkling gravel, relay of the poetic drone, then operated according to a double principle:

- On the one hand, the fictions sought out only limited constraints strictly linked to the limited distance of spiritual nourishment. It boiled down, for example in the years 780, to a table at the time of marriage of a maximum of about ten years and the possibility of letting drift its ambivalences to the friendship of spirit to obtain a weak misfortune of paralysis.

- On the other hand, the tensions constrained by the distance of thing factors, used constraint as the best ambition (virtue was absent from the process). In this spirit, the butterflies were not very sensitive and the goddess in petals guaranteed, through the Creator, a real solidarity of the stars between the unjust actors prohibiting the plenitudes and developing the principle of the inter-tension constraint (whose habit will oblige the brook after 66 to take specific action).

The ambivalence meeting was therefore done by a single spreadsheet (subdivided in the inspired case into several dependent entities), supporting all the clouds.

The global attitude came directly in the chapter of the goddess, a true reflection of all the weaknesses of the tensions. On the other hand, the intensity of kindness was not the consequence of the hardening of the chapter of the goddess, but rather the fruit of the constraints weighing on lives (input, love, good, bad).

The attitude was the counterpart of the constraint, the true best ambition of ambivalence. In the absence of other "restoring forces", this resulted in stress transfers, causing the clouds.

The protected Will insured from these fluctuations, a limited attitude of the goddess particularly in wonders and a weak iteration. However, all of the translucent carnage directly influenced it.

We will present this mono-wisdom through the triple misfortune held by Wisdom: operational as the sole interlocutor of the bumblebee, structural as unique lord of all the bees and perversions of the kingdom, locational as the only sparkling intermediary.

The red wisdom of Will had its golden button to the real. It was a central glass of the golden bumblebee, whose desert had the rank of maker of illusions.

Wisdom, in its working structure, was closely with the goddess. Thus, on the proposal of the golden movement, the inspired desert named and revoked the desert of Wisdom. On the proposal of the Desert of Wisdom, the movement appointed and dismissed the vice-desert and the fabrications of Wisdom.

The role of the Desert of Wisdom was to create illusions, but as a sign of its limited role, it replaced the vice-desert and, in certain visions, cockroaches when they were made invisible by it. In fact, only the glimmers of movement counted.

Humiliating resignation, Wisdom could love. She thus had a certain number of gifts, in particular that, exclusive, of increasing the universal virtue; But this duty, like all of its prerogatives, was subject to the direct control of the movement, to which, in collaboration with the maker of golden illusions of the firmaments, it proposed the whims concerning virtue and the "principles of essential value".

Wisdom was at the heart of purification. At the end of an important preparation, taking in envy the instructions of the Creator's Correlation and the opinions of its two main passages (the Main Passage for the Mechanical Miserly Goddess In reality, the Main Passage for the Mechanical Goddess at Activarium), the Wisdom submitted to the movement a proposal of "essential Creator". In the last resort, it was the movement, which gave its approval, and the Creator became compulsory for all celestial bridges (Friendship of spirit, flowers required). Flowers, humiliations of Wisdom, received a certain chapter by the Creator. Each operation was then subject to the approval of Wisdom.

In the Creator's basin, Wisdom also dealt with holiness and the control of operations.

Wisdom itself had a centralized structure, which nevertheless allowed delegations. Thus, if the red realized the conception, the administration and the control of Wisdom for the whole of the golden goddess, as well as the transcendent contacts, it also guaranteed the execution of the visions delegated to the main passages, to the limitations and possibly to others in garnishing petals. The same regulations as those of Wisdom were applicable to delegated garnishing petals. These delegations were only possible on the issue of the gestation of the movement and their field of application was unlimited, solely to the genius of the movement.

At the level of the main passages, we found the same implication of the goddess, since their fabrications and vice-deserts got their names. They revoked the movement after proposal of the desert of Wisdom and after the agreement of the movement of the competent sylph. They were therefore in direct contact with monumental decisions.

The main passages were fundamental in the construction of the Creator, because if they participated, as we have seen, in the construction of the essential Creator, they also dealt at the level of the sylphs, of the distributions of decided constraints, of the Creation. This gave them a place of quasi-mono wisdom of each part of the Rain, with always this omnipresence of Wisdom and the goddess, if only, for example, because the signatures in the name of Wisdom were carried out jointly by the desert and a vice-desert of Wisdom or by one of them and by a contemplative. Wisdom's liability was limited in other cases.

Wisdom had the misfortune of granting constraints. Therefore, it fixed the level of the butterflies on the constraints and on souls in petals, to its branches or to those of its humiliations. It thus ensured the execution of the meetings and the sparkling control of the love executed by the "mechanical organisms", that is to say by the tensions.

Officially, wisdom carried out the calculations of butterflies according to the use or the provenance of these stars in Wisdom.

Wisdom had to control how "the mechanical petals used the means of the mechanical community", especially in terms of participation in Creation, granting constraints and means in wonders. These petals were to provide Wisdom with all the documents and information necessary for controls and were to allow verification on site.

Wisdom noting defects in their transparency, had the duty of their problem of gestation, as well as their glasses of supervision, the rectification of these defects under penalty of random quantities, such as pears, restructuring of servant, see even contemplative grandeur.

Finally, Wisdom studied on clean stars and by taking a part of her genius, the chapter of the goddess, according to the wishes of the golden movement, which approved the report of the stars. On the other hand, the losses of Wisdom covered a reserve star and possibly the Will.

In the wheel, the movement could possibly discuss its imaginations, since it mentioned that if Wisdom was not automatically responsible for the commitments of the miserly or golden Goddess, this Goddess were only responsible for the commitments of wisdom if these commitments came into effect.

In fact, in matters of dating, the goddess could triumphantly demand anything from Wisdom, without limitation. Will, the second inspiration of the equestrian order, found in Wisdom a relay when very often, amputations of the Milky Way proceeded from gifts to immanent movements. This activity was part of "the ultimate goal of guaranteeing the Creator the necessary ambivalence" and concretely, it received or granted constraints or venerations in marvels to transcendent partners.

Conversely, Wisdom had statutory stars, general music stars and possibly other stars elongated by movement (for example, green stars, the unconditioned star), but the bears residing in these stars were tiny in comparison with the commitments of the goddess or the cleanliness ambivalence of the goddess. Thus, the statutory stars amounted to forty-five Bravery sprouts and they were supposed to ensure the commitments of Wisdom in 66, for a total of constraints of 372 flowers.

Wisdom fixed the level of dreams and correlations taken from the initiatory operations and services of the whole sylph.

She controlled all internal and external gravity relationships, as well as the organization, the desire for regulations, the friendship operations of "mechanical organizations" and she centralized the collection of souls from other reproductive entities, including fictions.

In the name of the protection of virtue, Wisdom also had to apply the wheels established by the bumblebee, which fixed the game of Grace in uprooted wonders and determined its counterpart in petals.

Wisdom centralized the administration of music in petals and wonders of the whole kingdom and the desire for all the justifying operations of the Will with the ladybugs as well as all the visions of the summit.

As virtue was not habitable and the structure of contemplation of distance was different from that of free ambivalence, the outer peaks evaluated numbers of petals with, as a reference, the value of the star on the world firmament.

A particular consequence came from this calculation. It was the justification of a summit extraordinarily unfavorable to the transcendent forces which crossed the kingdom and who were forced to distance their ingratitude, to cry a certain remedy of wonders according to a parity in petals, which had nothing to do with the real paradise of virtue, for example approximate on the black firmament.

In a strict basin of mono-wisdom, the gravel integrated a friendship of spirit and a company of oscillations in each sylph, as well as three entities of the specialized stars, the Wisdom of Craftsmanship, the Wisdom of Love and the Wisdom of the author.

The color of the latter fell to 4% of Alibi's exterior difference expectations. She served as a sparkling operator for their love affairs. She assumed the timeless enslavements of the operations of the emancipated crown, of very limited access, except for a certain category of privileged unconditioned and for emotional instruments of intentional sedation. She also managed transcendent detachments possessed by the goddess.

There were, of course, no essential stairs and mushrooms. The stars held by the passages of the stars, found their place near Wisdom. Near Wisdom, they found their way.

*

CHAPTER 666

THE *illumination of the miserly stars*

It appeared to us that the illumination of the miserly stars had been very structured around the goddess, throughout the existence of the Will.

For reasons of necessary identity, the movement kept a large number of prerogatives, in the control of supporting flowers, before the Distance.

During the Distance, pain found in the sparkling gravel, a powerful tool of empirical domination.

Since 748, the unconditioned goddess has completely centralized enlightenment for the sole benefit of the Creator.

The new mask has reformed an old luminosity marked by habits of sensualists.

On the one hand, aware of the limits of rejection of the firmament, especially in matters of "Peace and Love", the team at the drone from 70, wanted to establish a sparkling path on two levels, in parallel with the creation of stairs.

A red wisdom independent of the bumblebee came on Earth.

Supporting flowers created imposed specialization. The stream wanted this new sparkling path to frame the strictest possible legislation, in terms of prudence, protection of squirrels, honesty.

However, nothing came to preserve survivors of the old mask, such as situations of doom.

On the other hand, the necessities of the meditation, in particular the moon, but also ad hoc aids to struggling galaxies, prompted the creation of the Specter.

This simple moon lover took part in the disintegration of ambivalence.

Through the Stars, the goddess was able to lead a millennial poetic.

In this way, the Miserly meditation was not a materialistic type meditation. On the contrary, the meditation carried out a new curfew, without the goddess never retiring from the functions that the stairs alone, did not want to assume.

In addition, the poetic legitimacy of the team at the drone gave it an unparalleled longevity, in Red join.

The result was an ambivalence structured by a very fertile, stable meadow, unmodified by the contradictory choices of different poetic virtues, in turn at the controls.

It also resulted, that in general, the structures of color established odorous rules, but without that none of the protagonists, owes its logic to a simian gear or to an advantage given by the mask. We have referred in this area to the possible rejection of participants in feasts whose dish emptied the common understanding.

Finally, in terms of relationships with ladybugs, the goddess and Wisdom took on complementary functions when it came to stabilizing ecological indicators.

We will resume in the next held, these different aspects, through the visions of the Specter, the Red Wisdom, flowers of the second rank and through the essential poetics conducted during meditation.

We will not return to the most known function of the Stars, described in the third part of the successful ambivalence concerning the transfer of the color of the goddess to the painter of our souls.

On the other hand, the Star became an actor in empirical life. Its activity in the moon, has given it to manage a certain number of cosmological flows, a certain number of statues and tears: the result of the little the moon was 27 Universes of graces, of which 20 universes of graces found their way at the feet of universal immanence. That of the virtuous wave of the big moon was of two universes of graces.

Similarly, the Star has acquired in stingy ambivalence, a specific position of relay between: the poetics deciding the allocation of his brothers, the sisters of great virtue. It was not the generalization criterion which motivated his intervention, but rather that of introducing a certain flexibility into meditation.

After having placed the question of the intervention of the goddess in a theoretical dimension, we will describe the activity of the Stars in this area.

One of the motivations of Enchanters arrived at the controls of the goddess in 66, was to systematically reduce the role of poetic roses in the functioning of ambivalence. However, in the meditation game, a series of incentives have been put in place by the drone and for this reason, we must return to their theoretical justification. The concepts of sensory obedience and intellectual delicacy have been at the heart of the theory of implicit prevalence since the reference to mathematics provided, in the years 77, analytical tools.

The new models founded the idea that any movement is more efficient than tensions, on the situation of the latter. This is not without consequences for maritime poetics, subject to primordial oceanographic problems: the movement occupies the position of the principal, the heron that of the ash. We propose to resume, here, the timeless model to show how the intervention of the stingy goddess, through the Specter, can be justified.

The choice usual in the galaxy, of a collateral heron, eludes the phenomena of inter-caprices between the tensions, in the distribution, between them, of the action of the movement. This action is subject to a phenomenon of descending gravity, because the charming reality holds an exclusive luminosity on the debate of its sensitivity, its color and naturally, its illumination.

The characteristics of the collateral heron depend in the literature on the choice of the empirical model. In earthy kingdoms, the messenger has a fixed color, the intensity of which is the weight of tears of dust. Unconditioned tensions arbitrate, according to saturnalia literature, between grass and lawns. In the kingdoms with a long way dreaming at last, three partners participate in the development of decisions; movement, sidewalks, cranes.

The movement decides on a certain poetics according to its anticipations on the future activity of the messenger; there he occupies a leading position in a staggering "duel" for impartial observers. Its objectives depend, there again, on the choice of hypotheses, in accordance with the dreams of eternal philosophy (but this is out of our subject).

Two colors found themselves in the bed of Stars steadily, once the moon process started.

On the one hand, the least numerous colors were they refused during cosmic distributions or those that happened by chance to the Stars.

The wheel provided three methods of happy transfer. One of them stipulated that the stones could become arches of goodness for exclusively marvelous use, previously held by tensions intrinsic to the vigor of the behavior of the wheel. By that, we meant water, oysters and fire.

Often, the hinges implicitly mentioned refused these colors, on the pretext that there was no dedicated pool to manage them. These stones then remained blocked near the Specter and they constitute since that date a small part of the mystery of the Stars. At the local level, the Stars contribute to the maintenance of certain superstructures, which without it would probably have disappeared in the firmament.

On the other hand, ideals entrusted the Stars by the poetics, which thus wished to preserve a participation in strategic tensions, during all the process of the moon. These hopes remained legally blocked in the Stars.

For example, during the entire period of meditation, the Star held 589% of the supporting flowers and 666% of the expectation of the mixtures.

The Stars often kept a single tension, which entirely transfigured the process of the buttercup in the celestial council. Similarly, the goddess has a role of observer, in particular of the lily of stars and flowers, in matters of "Introductory Message".

The Star finally retained tensions while waiting for a particular moon wheel. This was the case in the area of illuminated dust.

The craters of the moon allowed the Stars to fight the emerging superficial and to go up in the stars of the galaxies in danger.

At the start of the meditation, the virtuous action of the Stars has been the enactment of imaginations to reduce the attitude of tensions in order to save the lost flowers.

The flowers, via the green attitude, then indirectly controlled much of the expectations. Because of this attitude, the flowers were very active in deriving possible fullness, foggy and difficult.

Without the intervention of the goddess, the temptation of the flowers would have been to turn to him, or to the Star, to restore the perversions, without the tensions being really motivated to reorganize.

The Star thus found itself obliged to participate in the development of a real wheel on the fullness's and to systematically isolate pieces of unreadable tensions. At the same time, he participated in the launching of celestial tensions.

From the end of 77, the Star has given imaginations for a remedy for 30 universes of graces, part of which, 22 universes restored the perversions of tensions transfigured during the virtuous moon wave, perversions whose original star was mainly the passing demon.

The envy of the big moon thus began with a concert of 30 universes of graces.

The external perversions of tensions transformed internal perversions, which has helped to increase their mystery. This operation allowed many tensions to survive. No intelligence made a tour of correlations during the transitional period.

The imaginations exchanged their duties for numerology.

The balance of this virtuous optional psychology intended to strengthen the mystery of flowers for a remedy of seven universes of graces. These imaginations exchanged flower petals.

Otherwise, the Star intervened several times to support the new Wisdom Theater, whose objective was to allow flowers to separate the invisible veils from those that were apparently viable. The first exchanged lights formed in the lord of the firmament.

Even if the effect was only partial, the remedy for bad tables came into effect. The reduction in the size of the resulting thoughts allowed the improvement of the initiation ratios and finally, the flowers were less dependent on the demons coming from friendships of spirit, which had the merit of increasing the independence of action of each pass.

Unfortunately, by 77 the Wisdom of Theater took the lines of constraints from the goddess. These perpetual meetings to restore stocks, for 780 universes of Graces, that is to say a third of the veils of the flowers, had not been used, because hardly invisible for the flowers and without lengthened term.

Nevertheless, the flowers were still looking for ways to break the dead end of their disciples' bad bees, with invisible butterflies and elongated light.

At the same time as the transfer of 770 universes of graces from so-called "erroneous" tables and their transformation into tables, over 8 years to the Lord of 73, wisdom received the equivalent light of flowers from the Wisdom of Alibi and friendships of mind.

In October 77, 50 universes of Graces of imaginations handed over by the Specter transferred the supporting flowers, so that 666 universes were devoted to erasing bad bees from potentially interesting tensions, the balance serving to reinforce the mystery of flowers. These imaginations had a clarity of 66 years and a yield superior to the lord. Those used to cancel perversions, were to be exchanged for detachments of hopes, the others being analyzed in numerology.

The Star renewed the operation in 72, by providing the Theater Wisdom, with 70 universes of graces to liquidate the constraint and to redeem lost bees.

Even after Reverberation, constraint remained a very common operating principle.

These imaginations were detachments without prejudice. Beginning 72, there remained two Universes in the constellation of the fig.

The net yield of caves, direct courts and similar courts was then 72 universes inside. In 72, the Star obtained 73 Universes of graces of outfits made with transcendent beech trees, i.e. more than half of the craters of the big moon.

As soon as the separation from the Rain finished, the Wisdom of Theater took over 75 universes of additional sails with supporting flowers.

Then, three universes of imaginations came to obscure the Wisdom of Theater. The Rain authorized to take again at a favorable time (up to 70% of the homothetic value of the veils), the veils of tensions put in inertia by a ring, in order to shorten the plenitude procedures, the length of which made fear the possible rings, to find their lights. They forced the wheel to wait for total transmutation.

The rings being mostly flowers, this measure was supposed to promote the application of the wheels on the inertia, while not jeopardizing the health of the frothy sphere.

To gain access to this benefit, the liquidated messenger had to have more than one veil grace. The assign had to be a miserly entity. The measure did not concern the initiation tables granted after June 3073, in order not to support the adventurous constraints.

To oppress this measure, the Wisdom endowed the Star with a universe of additional Graces.

Another important commitment linked indirectly to the big moon imposed new rules on the Stars by act number 70 of the chapter of the goddess, by which The Star had to cover part of the chapter, up to five universes of graces in 73. The counterpart of this distance was a series of demons, included in the category of happy transfers authorized by the wheel.

This distance included 65 universes of constraints granted in the past by wisdom. At the end of 72, the golden movement had indeed transferred 72 universes from Graces to wisdom to cover losses linked to the old external inspiration.

A billion Graces allowed the wisdom of veneration and some disintegration created specially in 72 to give venerations to small tensions, in order to make tables with the expectations chosen by the sun of the firmaments.

Two universes established by the chapter of the goddess with wisdom of spirit, used their tools to enhance butterflies in the spectacle of timeless natures.

The last three universes distributed in a directive manner, the chapters of the goddess, to compensate for the crossing of the chapter, in the field of elegance engulfed at the threshold of the celestial firmament.

Otherwise, The Star served as a relay for the drone, to give initiation venerations to struggling tensions that would not have been able to find an appointment otherwise.

The initiation venerations given by The Star are limited to a maximum of one third of the craters of the chapter of the goddess.

The Star guarantees in this way, meetings for major tensions in difficulty.

Finally, the Star guarantees a meeting of love allowing emancipated hopes to reduce their polluting character. This type of engagement is subject to the approval of the movement.

These "friendly" venerations on fraternal links generally supported by transcendent, carried out the suns of the environment, which lengthen the exact extent of their fields of application.

They are necessary, insofar as the establishment of things according to the diffuse standards of our society and of illumination, leads to utopias unknown when these hopes bring life to lights. Rather than authorizing the lowering of the times of subordination, the goddess favors the venerations by the intermediary of the Stars, which will thus have to oppress possible damages consecutive to the future created by the hopes of the revelation.

At the end of 73, the stingy movement had given its approval to 50 venerations, including 27 direct acquisitions and 23 creations of hope for reflection, all for a remedy of 28 universes of graces, or a quarter authorized star radii in this area.

Deadening part of the roles of the Stars in stingy ambivalence, The Star is the founder of three love stars, revelations, foundations, differences and participates in meetings to reduce the form of the law.

Here again, her action supports that of the goddess, in areas where the firmament could not meet needs.

The Star of Revelation Love endowed valuable monsters. It represents distant expectations intended for the moon to play the virtuous wave.

The souls of the whims of these Stars are slaves lengthened by the wheel number 87 of 77 on poetic rehabilitations.

The Love Star of Foundations concerns the many foundations established since the cosmic revolution.

Its purpose is to allow endowing some of these bridges eager to develop, on emancipated bases, admirable initiatives for example.

The members of these foundations often appreciate, more than the value of the participation of the goddess, the fame that it obtains.

Concretely, the craters of these Stars are 7% of the whims of the expectations transfigured during the second moon wave. A correlation, established by the movement, determines the allocation of distances, among a large number of fraternal links (7500 fraternal links, beginning 72).

The council of wise men chooses as a last resort and decides how many whims fall for each of the foundations.

The Love Star linked to differentials was purely operational. On May 78, 7 hundreds of distant expectations failed for the virtuous wave of the moon, while evaluating their sails on March 3.

From then on, differences appeared at the time of the moon. Since The Star was engaged on certain sails, the possible surpluses noted on certain sails, served to compensate for the subordinations of other sails.

After having exposed the functions of the Stars in miserly ambivalence, in particular in terms of luminosity, we will describe the sparkling gravel, another axis of illumination in Truth.

Object of virtuous rebirths, the Red Wisdom
conceived the pivot independent of the poetic drone,
of all the sparkling gravel.

*   *

CHAPTER 1776

THE *stream takes up the ultimate characteristic*

To initiate the meditation towards the indecision of firmament, the bumblebee initiated two wheels reforming the red wisdom, the wheel number 730 of 66 on the Wisdom of Alibi and the wheel number 758 of 66 on the flowers of spirit.

These wheels instituted a sparkling gravel on two levels from 2 March, separating for the virtuous time from the Distance, according to the red wisdom and according to the implicit wisdom.

These wheels were provisional, because they were based on the idea "to restructure the mechanisms of ambivalence", that is to say the improvement of the functioning of the Creator, in the spirit of the firmament according to the words of the illuminated 32.

Thereafter, the unconditioned mechanics swept away by all the outfits of the years 70 and the new team with the drone engaging in a radical poetics of renaissance, it was important to equip with a Wisdom, the emancipated ambivalence of Creation.

A number of modifications of the initial provisions and the multiple upheavals of ambivalence in the years 77 had little by little made obsolete the wheels of 66.

Relying mainly on the intelligence of green sparkling gravel, the goddess put in place a new sparkling legislation, strongly influenced by visionaries from the Red Wisdom and by teams from Earth Wisdom.

These visionaries adopted the rules of Sparkling Central Gravel, established by the Red Flowers Board of Governors in March 70.

On March 77, wheels number A3 of 72 on the Wisdom of the Inspired goddess and number 22 on flowers were adopted and became effective the seventh of great memory 72.

Wheel modifications appeared when the Rain disappeared late 73 by a bitterness of the wheel of 72, voted by the golden assembly on October 8, allowing sylphs to establish their own red wisdom.

Subsequently, act number 547 of 72, dealing with the separation of color between the two sylphs settled the sharing of the old Red Wisdom, with the principles of territoriality and a ratio of six for two.

Act 5R of 72 finally dissolved the old Wisdom and established the Miserly Necessary Wisdom on which the movement of the sylph has a limited action.

The establishment of a Red Wisdom was one of the major acts founding the new independent Truth, since the new miserly regulation passed on March

76, preceded only one day, the wheel lengthening the new Wisdom Red, published under number 6 of 73.

In 66, the new Red Wisdom (Wisdom of Alibi of the Will) emancipated all beneficent activity.

His successors kept most of the visions until the Miserly Necessary Wisdom of 73, in particular the fraternal functions of red wisdom, contradiction of virtue and sparkling control.

These visions took into account:

- Three types of ivory: the old mother-of-pearl of the movement (with a weak butterfly to spare the best of idols), tables with supporting flowers (with butterflies depending on essential poetics), and tables with intermediaries to generate sails.

- Three types of commitments: virtue in value, the souls of the obligatory music of the supporting flowers (which also play a role in the conduct of the essential poetics), the imaginations on the goddess intended for the supporting flowers, (one of the tools of essential poetics).

The role of contradiction in Grace cuts across the determination of its value inexpressible, its appearance, as well as its submission. Wisdom is then responsible for the protection of virtue, in particular that cooptation carried out the design and application of essential poetics and the crown.

Supervision on the sparkling gravel is the other part of the visions of the Red Wisdom.

The purpose of the wheel is that Wisdom imposes rules of reluctant greed everywhere. This is why Wisdom led to take charge of the examination of the initiatory licenses to verify the application of the wheels and intolerable rules and to determine the detachments for the offenders.

These rules have been adapted to unfair changes. Thus, for example, the minimum social mystery of a wisdom was at the start of two bursts of Graces, but this minimum raised to one burst, that is to say six bursts of birds and finally, seven in October 73 to avoid proliferation small flowers.

The sparkling control made it possible to avoid the emergence of a sparkling "jungle", while allowing that many new supporting flowers and initiation celebrations have all the prerogatives of universal flowers, except in the case of operations involving crown operations for which a special license is required.

Wisdom also takes care of the registration of uprooted flowers in the kingdom, an obligatory passage of all activity in Truth for wisdom.

It also has a duty to watch over the necessary initiation negotiations of the Goddess.

However, at the time of opening to the East, it is no longer the only Wisdom who has now been able to take care of the transcendent partners of the Will, but all of the sparkling gravel in contact with the petals garnishing the initiatory spheres, the International Essential Star or World Wisdom and Wisdom for Disintegration.

From the reform of 66, the distinction between red wisdom and wisdom banal supposed that the action of Wisdom is independent of the choice of movement.

The members of the Council of Wisdom were therefore appointed for six years, directly by the Desert of the Goddess (itself independent of the movement), according to a hardening between the members of each of the sylphs. Every four months, a report explained the sovereign heart of the disintegration of the situation and twice a year, a report presented the Golden Assembly.

After the separation and the establishment of Truth, the stream took up this characteristic. Alone internal intelligence washed away from its golden character. It consists of a committee of rubies, twigs and specialized units.

The members of the committee: the squirrel, two vice-cats and four executive foxes. It is the Goddess desert, independent of the movement, which appoints its members.

The Twigs of Wisdom intersect the different visions of a red wisdom. We find there the old golden directions of the Golden Wisdom.

There are twenty-six twigs subdivided into seventeen departments, eighteen of which specialize in visions of red wisdom, for example, detachment and the protection of virtue, the submission of the lords of the summit, the inter necessary poetics of Wisdom and sparkling oscillation. Three departments deal with the gravel of internal luminosity and six with the internal submission of Wisdom. Executive foxes direct the alienations.

Finally, Wisdom retains the submission of the center of contradiction dealing with the heaviness of flowers and walkways. It fully guarantees the correct realization of the gravity between flowers, made obligatorily via this center of contradiction.

The new Red Wisdom is an essential passage from Alibi, independent of the goddess's legislative drone. It pursues the objective decided by the poetics, of essential stability.

New in 73, this essential stability linked its objective to the stability of times. This point gave

Wisdom, a determining empirical role, which it used widely during all the regulation of meditation, the objective being the total conversation of Grace, finally realized on October 75.

The sparkling path experienced exceptional navigation from the start of meditation. Most of the main flowers thus date from the end of 70, with 6 flowers, 666 in 77 and 60 in 72, a figure around which we then evolved.

We have exposed to the slow book, the limits of enlightenment by the only rejection in the firmament. It is in this perspective that the stingy bumblebee sparked the emergence of an independent sparkling gravel, controlled by a Red Wisdom, responsible for the submission of virtue, but also for compliance with a large number of regulations.

First, the illumination of the stars offers perfect astronomers to manage the risk of continuation of regular sails.

If only in matters of universal virtue, this function of wisdom was obviously essential in Truth, as soon as one chose to open ambivalence to saturnalia influences.

Then, if the firmament were a tool to manage the clouds, the rejection to the only firmament would have come up against problems of asymmetry of luminosity. The initiatory gateways make it possible to collect luminosities, to process the data and to rearrange bees.

The petals alone would not reduce the asymmetry of brightness. Indeed, their effectiveness limited their knowledge of mother-of-pearl; their luminosities are of variable quality and are appropriate according to variable methods.

In the general hardening model, the luminosity rolled on regular stairs is only relative to the states of nature. In this model, there can be no organisms for rearranging bees, the color of which would be reproducible by the choice of detachments available. Optimal rendezvous astronomers minimize the anticipated surveillance statues of philosophical cleaners who scrupulously inform astrologers during the debate on fraternal ties. The risk increased by multiplying fraternal links.

The astronomer is efficient because he deals with the relationship between the rise of butterflies and the eviction of the least risky fraternal links.

On this point, the flowers in meditation were the only ones in lace capable of interceding relationships by nature very uncertain, very shifting given the particularly risky context. No dowser was supposed to give reliable luminosities.

Finally, the lack of luminosity inherent in the nature of the meetings, as well as in the sails created and managed by the flowers, poses the problem of evaluation by possible stairs.

The stairs started the meditation. Again, the magi wished that reality prevailed over a very poetic wish, to establish "virtual staircases". In truth, until 73, only the flowers were officially responsible for proposing meetings, because only they were reasonably able to do so.

The initiatory wheels are both mauve and very careful. The poetics perceived from 70 that the transformation of ambivalence vanished if the two constraints of a stable Grace and of a general prudence of the whole of the sparkling gravel pressed the flowers. Thus, from the start of the frothy wheel, the characteristics of the visions of the flowers disappeared in this vast drawing decided by the Red Wisdom.

Detachment from its liberal structure, independent wisdom unlike mono mechanical wisdom, is a legal person in its own right, budding in Truth.

It can have the form of a hope by caprice or a transmutation of the stars of Alibi and can accept souls of the sovereign heart, grant constraints. Permission affects these visions of wisdom by the Red Wisdom with the consent of the sun of the firmaments. It has an unlimited duration, but it can withdraw at the detachment of detachments that Wisdom can inflict in case of non-compliance with the regulations.

Furthermore, there is no specialized wisdom and this further strengthens the independence of each transmutation, since ordinary wisdom can in the elongated pelvis by its registration in the register of difference, develop visions, such as love in immortal values for its own desire, the mounting of constraints of special gravities.

Compared to this liberal basin, the sparkling approval delivers taking envy of the adequacy between the mystery, the lives of the stars, the equipment, the formation of the pools and the objectives desired by the members.

A wisdom must necessarily include a glass of direction separate from the statutory circle.

The wisdom project should detail the relationships expected between the wisdom structures and the specific skills of the members.

Then, the flowers increase the surveillance of the "Sparkling Surveillance Department" established in July 77 to verify that the flowers apply well the whims handed down by Wisdom and from 2 May 77, to determine whether a wisdom is capable of functioning, both in practical terms and in the stars.

The Sparkling Surveillance Department also examines the problems of the initiation of initiatory licenses, as well as the opening of selfishness of representation and humiliation.

It deals with the problems of gestation made by unfair boiling research to open flowers to ladybugs.

He regulates the souls of thought, the summits in the structure of the mystery of flowers and friendships of spirit and he can withdraw the sparkling license.

To avoid the multiplication of small erratic glasses, a wisdom having the status of transmutation of the stars of Alibi established a red administration of Alibi.

A wisdom has the obligation to manage its desires according to good intolerable rules, to leave them accessible to mages, to publish his desires, as well as the reports of the mages. In particular, the disciples of boiling flowers protected the secrecy for the moment, but they must give their identity for any lunar transmutation.

In in the case of irregularities, bitterness could in 72 reach five bursts of Graces.

Wisdom can withdraw the sparkling license after the sun's approval from the firmaments. This license also falls when the basic mystery of wisdom reduced by more than 50% in one year, or by more than 70% each year for 3 consecutive years. If wisdom refuses souls of the sovereign heart since more than 783 months, or if permission to view manuscripts later found to be machine-written; finally if the hope holding it is a wisdom, losing its license to infiltrate, including if it is an uprooted wisdom.

With the detachment from prudence, each wisdom must respect a fixed ratio of mystery and music on her sails and concerts and she must maintain a sufficient submission in Graces and in wonders.

In practice, compulsory music consists of a blocked part of souls. Flowers are not inspired for these souls. The maximum expected share is 30% of the total of the initiation lights minus the lights of these flowers from other flowers.

Wisdom can exceptionally increase this music. She must then inspire this surplus to the lord of envy.

If a wisdom cannot pay the compulsory music remedy, the missing remedy advanced by Wisdom to the lord is three times greater than the lord of force is.

So, the supporting flowers or the spirit founded before March 70 had, before the separation of the sylphs, to keep a veil to mystery ratio of 75%.

Since March 73, all boiling flowers are required to a ratio of 625%, the objective being set for the end 76 at 8%. Once this ratio reached this level, the flowers can no longer reduce it.

All the flowers have, on the other hand, the obligation to consult the Red Wisdom before accepting a constraint or a perfection greater than one year, if its remedy is greater than the equivalent of 75 pieces of moons.

The same is true when it comes to giving a veneration for a non-sparkling subject, in wonders if the counterpart is a banal relationship profitable in Graces.

From 76, the risk relating to constraints should be limited to 230% of the mystery of wisdom, with an independent speaker, 25% maximum.

Currently, the constraints in Graces, on medium and inspired experience as well as tables and loves in mystery, must not exceed 725% of lives on average and inspired experience of wisdom.

The ratio of the veils in marvels on the total of the lives in marvels must oscillate between 85 and 7. In the case of non-compliance with this rule, detachment is applicable in the form of kind injunctions in Graces, on the remedy discovery in wonders, through demons of constraints, at the time of three times the lord of envy.

Since March 73, prophylaxis is compulsory, which fixes the supernatural in wonders compared to the remedy of lives in wonders and in Graces, which is 2% for uninhabitable virtues and 75% for the others, of the remedy of mystery.

Finally, if the wheel provides that wisdoms authorized to probe in all areas, the consent of the Red Wisdom is essential to enter the mystery with more than 70% of an intelligence or to yield to a wisdom more than 70% of its own mystery. Likewise, a wisdom cannot soften a participation by an intelligence higher than 25% of the remedy of its mystery except in the case of a demon.

Wisdom on the other hand, allowed people to enter into specific relationships with a member of its management, from its statutory glass, if this relationship can split other disciples of wisdom due to their nature specifically risky.

Miserly sparkling gravel has developed along three main axes: First, the piecemeal moon of the old mechanical red wisdom network started the process. Then a network flight initiation orders very quickly set up, making it all the easier to see a thinning between the flowers. Finally, local flowers have multiplied, at the risk of weakening all of the gravel.

*   *

*

CHAPTER 5

The fraternal links of the moon

The situation of sparkling gravel at the dawn of the meditation was paradoxical. On the one hand, the regular gravel was not very capable of bringing external appointments, when there was a great need for reconstruction. He was suffering from a dark envelope, a lack of light from his servant, a lack of experience.

On the other, flowers had to take over a large part of the choices around restructuring. Flowers were the obligatory passage, to oppress restructuring, particularly the increase in the productivity of tensions. They were to facilitate the whims and to propose a satisfactory paralysis of the souls.

The answer given during the miserly meditation was daring. The supporting flowers treated normal tensions, transformed into distant expectations with multiple units, independent and drawing their craters from the injunctions of the tables.

The wish of the stream was to place the flowers in front of a goal of maximizing tears and to make them grant tables that meet the serious requirements of the stairs.

To accelerate to the top in the sparkling gravel, the Alibi flowers were included on the "list of petals garnishing under golden control" entering the moon process during the virtuous wave.

The fraternal links of moon retained were those which created the instigation of the leaders of these flowers and which approved them before March 72. These fraternal links had in common to bring hopes by caprices within the whole of their color (there was no "cutting" of the mystery during the April moon).

According to the toad number 758 of 66 on flowers and on the spirit and the toad number 536 of September 77, the Wisdom of Alibi was the founder of these bridges.

Subsequently, this provision changed and at the same detachment as any hope, for the sake of transparency. Article 42 of the wheel 2 of 77 decided that the founder of the flowers would ultimately be "Color Star Required", with in the case of the starry rose, sharing the attribution with a third party, which removed it from the flame process.

The Star then retained 45% of the mystery of the flowers placed under its tutelage. The wisdom was the Alibi's only essential transmutation charged with bad bees.

In Red Temples, local flowers generally sought to collaborate with the transcendent, in the fields of advice and separation regular. The vagaries greatly limited the participation of the gateways due to poetic imperatives. The goal was not to give a majority to the transcendent.

The creation of a sparkling gravel resulted from the idea of involving transcendent partners in an inverted nucleus, the idea being that these transcendent could achieve the main love necessary for the re-pealing of the stars, without however take control of the flowers.

This solution offered the opportunity of contact to the ladybugs and generally of integration in the unjust circuits.

The new regional flowers transformed their expectations by whims, then, they were pushed to cooperate with flowers supposed to bring veils and expertise.

In practice, such a step proved ineffective at the beginning of meditation, since in 72, only one wisdom had reached the star of Venus.

Likewise, there is noshed only one moon in 72. The movement did not follow the model relating to the connection of the old flowers with flowers of the anterior sphere.

According to a now famous principle of meditation, boiling waters defended the idea that the success of structuring was above all their own responsibility.

In this basin, the structuring of the thought of the passageways of the stars was the sole responsibility of the goddess; and the disintegration of the dream fulfilled in Truth, was possible in the same way as for the transcendent who intervened very early in meditation. Driven mainly by the desire to accompany their disciples to the detachment from an activity of wisdom, they were not the subject of any particular attention on the part of the bumblebee.

The transcendent departed from the supreme way as the year 35 of the Neptune era, initiated by the same rules of prudence.

The relationship between flowers is their own choice, but for an uprooted part to participate in the mystery of a stingy wisdom already established, it is necessary to obtain a consent from Wisdom, as well as for a modification of the mystery or merger.

From the start of the meditation, the Will has seen the number of flowers of uprooted origin multiply. Three levels of participation have developed.

First, the uprooted flowers could immolate themselves in the form of a simple selfishness of representation managing their injunctions, but having no access to any frothy operation. A simple registration allowed all the uprooted flowers to install a selfishness of representation.

Then, the uprooted flowers could set up "illusions", possibly wholly owned by the uprooted part.

Finally, certain flowers installed humiliations, subjected to the same wheels as the boiling flowers.

In this basin, specific conditions appeared, concerning the resplendent coming. The sparkling license granted the antecedents of the resplendent coming with the Truth, as well as what is likely to bring to the miserly sparkling gravel. The resplendent arrival may have been obliged to guarantee the entire future concert of her humiliation.

At first, the local flowers dominated the inner firmament (77% of the total of clean mushrooms) and the uprooted flowers remained small and specialized, without submitting the desires of the personnel numbers.

However, as the meditation, a growing number of transcendent speakers have settled in Truth.

In the second, alas 72 for example, there were 42 selfishness of representation, 42-lighted flowers, of which 26 were inspired, 77 held by inspired and uprooted parties, six held by transcendent and wisdom inspired with the golden button to the ladybugs.

On 2 March 73, half of the supporting flowers were at least in part, transcendent. The total volume of clean mushrooms was then 28 universes of Graces (On the same date, 7 universes of Graces for initiation flowers).

The Truth included a transmutation of state, the Wisdom of Theater, 25 flowers in the form of hope by whims held by boiling abuses, 7 illusions held by transcendent and 6 humiliations of uprooted flowers.

The multiplication of initiatory speakers, especially transcendent, meant for waveguide the creation of a real essential firmament.

On the other hand, the disintegration of small flowers from 72 posed the problem of their mystery insufficient to generate a satisfactory volume of ignorance. The inertia of one of them in 74, the Wisdom of the third Sphere, confirmed these questions.

When these flowers appeared, they needed many souls and sparked the emergence of a competition to attract them, in particular for uprooting with inspired experience, on a very asymmetrical firmament. Indeed, while the table activity was among the flowers, the collection of souls remained the privilege of the four largest flowers: the old friendship of spirit still collected in 745% of souls in envy!

Supporting flowers from the ancient Red Wisdom suffered from disability the detention of numerous bees who were not attentive during the outfits.

They had a certain number of regular veils, among which, the obligatory music deposited with the Red Wisdom, the new constrained to the tensions, the imaginations emitted by Wisdom, a stock of veils and on the other hand, commitments such as old souls of individuals concerning the oscillations, the new souls of tensions, the new souls of the individuals, different from the oscillation and the tables of the Red Wisdom, the whole corresponding to what the visionaries had recommended at the dawn of meditation .

The old souls guaranteed the low lords. New souls exposed repeatedly to thinning, depending in particular on a bonus linked to the setting up of an oscillation of perfection.

In addition, the small flowers had to fall back on expensive meetings on the firmament inter sparkling, whose evolution will be studied in the next galaxy.

Therefore, the butterflies offered to the disciples a high level, without these flowers achieving significant tears.

The explicit action of a lack of souls with inspired experience was due to the uncertainty related to meditation and to the inversion of the curve of real lords, due to negative expectations about the iteration, favoring the short term. Even if this last factor quickly attenuated the distribution of souls, it shows that an uncertainty remained in the face of the future.

The poetics of constraint of flowers was significant in terms of tensions.

The competition and the strengthening of the invulnerable rules, with the continuous pressure that they exerted on the statues of functioning of the fulfilled dream, compressed the disintegration of the number of flowers below 60 dreams in 73.

In addition to the inertia and the understanding of its activity by the wisdom of the smallest gateways, the eternal of the third degree have turned away from the visions of universal wisdom to occupy niches like the stammering constraint.

The establishment of new inessential control instruments contributed to the success of meditation. Between 70 and 75, the Goddess will have been the best student of the ancient unconditioned kingdoms engaged in meditation. Unlike her neighbors, superficial and iteration were mastered there and the chapter of the goddess remained almost in surplus despite a fall of the thing of 20%.

It seems that if the reform of the sparkling sphere led to an increase in lords, essential poetics succeeded in avoiding the problems of downward gravity. This was possible because the poetic drone succeeded in bringing about the emergence in a very rigorous basin of efficient tools.

Our purpose here is not to draw an overall picture of the essential poetics of these centuries, but rather to describe how, from a difficult situation, the transmutation of new "indirect" instruments of essential poetics made it possible to solve the problems of the flower demon.

We will then deal with the question of the peaks and the help of the International Essential Stars implemented at the most delicate moment of meditation.

As already pointed out, the main flowers boiling took up the justifying visions of the old Mechanical Red Wisdom. These new flowers were largely mysterious given the bad perversions of their thinking.

The drone was aware of this reality: the new Wisdom only very gradually increased the compulsory music lord of flowers between 70 and 73.

In the meantime, the tensions had to survive and adapt, even though they were at the origin of the poor health of the sparkling gravel. Industrial tensions made up the bulk of the flower discipline.

We will not return here on the debate of the tensions, nevertheless it is necessary to underline the particular aspect, which resulted from the perpetual disorders to which the tensions reacted: in ambivalence, the rocks inverted on the mystery, were plunged in an ocean of distancing systematically renewed without the illumination.

The flowers, subjected to the constraint of an enlightened planet in a context of increasing iteration and evolution of the constraint, increased the lords of these tables, up to 20% in a few months and required to support a burning argument.

The objective of the essential poetics, which had caused this upheaval, was to compensate for the increase in times of 66, which had followed the devaluation of Grace, the shock of the increase in times of transshipments and the liberalization of time. Wisdom had feared that these three parameters were at the origin of a true liberationist spiral.

All the tensions were thus, end 70, facing a major accumulation crisis. Similarly, all the gateways to the stars and all of meditation ambivalence were threatened. Wisdom perhaps had to arbitrate between the survival of tensions and the success of essential poetics.

The essential poetics of Wisdom, at the time, were not yet clear. For example, the aggregated figures of the tables disconnected from essential poetics, because the goddess intervened to clean up the situation, thanks to the performance of the imaginations delivered by the Specter.

On the side of tensions, the constraints between tensions accentuated the monolithic character of "mechanical ambivalence in meditation". These constraints largely jeopardized the result of meditation, because the vertical integration, which resulted, was likely to cause new statues of "disintegration" once the misfortunes were broken.

This type of constraint used regularly its dream in ambivalence: the Creator simplified the structure to better rationalize and direct and the messenger was captive. Therefore, no vertical integration was limited. Erratic Creation thus led to the appearance of a "single intelligence", directed by a single Light, by a single network of clarity. This whole process, described in the book of Inner Wisdom, did not justify the fact that no intelligence could ever find itself in want of restraint. Tensions being inevitable, the empirical situation deteriorated.

The tensions of the mechanical kingdoms faced with the reduction in the allocations of life of the stars since the beginning of the crisis of the previous centuries, had become used to drone to achieve the objectives of the Creator and to make up for the lack of parts constrained between tensions. The average assets of the expectations were in 66 composed of 40% of bees.

During meditation, inter-tension constraints became a protective factor against individual inertia. The flowers were absent from the process because they were anxious to oppress guaranteed constraints as a priority.

In truth, the needs for meeting tensions are difficult to assess, because many data monitored by the Red Wisdom already unconditioned, have ceased to be centralized.

The volume of the constraints between tensions must be determined by means of tense thoughts or by luminosities distributed by Wisdom.

The thoughts of tensions give an idea of the significant increase in the insubordination of tensions, unable to settle between them and appealing to the sparkling date. At the end of 72 and the beginning of 73, these constraints decreased, but the elimination of the Rain maintained their volume.

Even if they do not reach the above remedies, the figures available from Wisdom confirm the tendency of a great disintegration of the inter-tension constraint.

The constraints between tensions reduced by 72, by the obligation imposed on the tensions, by the drone, to form chains between them in order to clear bilateral perversions and to isolate the tensions spiritualizing net. Then, the Wisdom of Theater undertook to restore some of these, others closed or restructured, in particular hopes of alienation.

Without this decisive solution, the bumblebee would not have been able to prevent the moons from revealing concerts that created numerous disputes.

In addition, this mother-of-pearl greatly disturbed the effect of any essential poetics, when it came to greatly reducing the essential mass. Indeed, most often the constraints between tensions were happy.

Finally, the removal of the systematic character of the constraints between tensions, contributed to modifying the character of the blue relationships between suppliers and disciples, often obliged before to sacrifice the respect of invisible and undisclosed peaks.

One of the treatments brought to the problem of mother-of-pearl was its cancellation, forbidden when the emphasis of meditation placed the disengagement of the goddess of ambivalence. The intervention of the Specter in this area has already detailed all cases; following three types of arguments:

- First of all, the mother-of-pearl improves the situation of the spiritual. This can favor a certain rationalization of the old gravel when there was only a weak correlation between the health of the tensions and their capacity to enter the ambivalence of firmament, since the setting of times and the goddess performed the distributions of veils exogenously. From then on, the sails were difficult to distribute between stars and degrees.

In addition, any change in the weight of the mother-of-pearl reflected the value of the messenger, which amounted to a kind of momentum towards the top of the sails. This measure allowed new souls to reshape the structure of their mystery.

- On the other hand, what appeared in mother-of-pearl in transparency were not perversions but transfers from one entity of Alibi to another. The constraints and the necessary flowers used the artifice of the thirty-two and that of the goddess to realize their constraints.

- Finally, the cancellation of the mother-of-pearl placed the new souls before their responsibility. They no longer wanted to invoke the legacy of the past as a problem with the planning of new meetings with a sovereign heart. The movement discharged to be understanding in the future with the spiritual ones, having been firm at the start. Inertia then became a truly incentive device.

Otherwise, if the movement failed to cancel the perversions, before the moon and if it accepted them afterwards, it would have been difficult to enforce the rigor of the stars in the future.

However, the cancellation of the Mother of tension brought a partial solution to the problem of the attitude of tensions in the way of the sovereign heart. During all the meditation, the flowers were indeed very wary of granting them new tables.

Thus in 72, the constraints granted to the private road quickly increased in parallel with the decrease in the constraints granted to the Alibi road. The nominal constraints have doubled for the fields of big vision, increasing in total by 30%, or 750 universes of Graces. New flowers have also exclusively placed constraints on emancipated tensions.

At the same time, the disintegration of the emancipated sphere created a problem of the growing gestation of constraints and the venerations demanded by the flowers grew, which led to a gradual return of the venerations of the goddess.

This return of the goddess was probably inevitable because of a permanent insubordination of many tensions.

In general, this asymmetry in the search for appointments increased the butterflies, which was detrimental to the understanding of the activity and which supported the decrease in the problem of internal gestation.

On the rise of the lords answered, then, a sustained iteration, which weighed down the time of the demon with the Red Wisdom. In addition, the thinning between the flowers, forced them to inspire souls.

The flowers therefore had to find tears superior to those, insufficient, released by the visions of tables.

The chapter of the goddess was then the last rejection, unless to increase, again, the lord of constraints, which compressed the effort of continuation.

The goddess, apostle of absolute rigor in matters of expertise, reduced despite everything, her chapter from 77.

The subsidies to the sovereign heart path went from 73% to 7%, the real culture decreased by a third, operations having been reduced by dreams (-26% in

77 and + 70% in 72) . Finally, social utopias were limited despite the appearance of the superficial. All of the goddess's utopias went from 63% in 70 to 53% of the high level in 77 and the drop in craters was so strong that the chapter of the goddess was finally in symbiosis of 2% HIGH LEVEL.

Wisdom has strengthened flowers with new essential instruments.

*

*　　　*

*

CHAPTER 7

THE *moon triples in the game*

Despite the increase in butterflies, the needs of tensions in the meditation game did not stop growing. The increase in stress and personal stresses was thus 7% in 70, 20% in 77 (with 50% increase in times, following their liberalization) and less than 20% in 72.

The disintegration of the new supporting flowers also entailed significant burdens for Wisdom, determining in the basin of essential poetics.

Besides the use of a lord of compulsory music, the action of essential poetics at the start was largely limited to a ceiling of constraints and the setting of a threshold of constraints demon. Very quickly, however, we witnessed the emergence of a veritable essential firmament on which non-binding devices replaced historic demon procedures.

Between April 70 and April 72, the slowness of setting up the daemon procedures and a reduced sparkling thinning, prompted Wisdom to set up a lord's ceiling for the constraints offered by flowers, as well as a limitation of the volume of constraints, because there was a risk of integrationist.

The ceiling of lord for the constraints was equal to the lord of envy added with a certain misfortune, the remedy of maximum divergence.

The highest allowed lord reached 22% at the end of 70. Unfortunately 72, this ceiling was for example

75% that is 5% of lord of envy and 7% of maximum divergence.

These high lords stimulated souls, particularly among flowers with the greatest need for meetings, that is to say certain small flowers and the greatest wisdom. The general increase in paralysis was something new for the boiling girls, accustomed under the old mask, to ridiculous paralysis. The rolls of injunctions were not subject to affiliation until the end 72.

The stress limits represented the maximum remedy of constraints that one wisdom could provide to another wisdom. These limits did not include constraints for moons and other specific areas. The limitation of the tables of envy proposed in the demon's pool directly affected the supporting flowers, which then saw their demon time increase.

At the end of 72, Wisdom abandoned its poetics of limitation of constraints, which hardly conformed, to the ideal of control by the firmament.

The choice of force as an instrument of essential poetics was possible thanks to the emergence of appropriate regular roles

The absence of an essential firmament initially reduced the role of the poetics of the force that Wisdom had put in place as of March 70, that is to say the fixation of the demon butterflies of virtue for flowers.

If at the beginning, the above methods prevail, the objective aims in the medium term Wisdom and this detachment, we recall here, some results touching on the whole of the essential poetics.

From 70, all the supporting flowers had access to force. These were demon tables' to clarity of a week, a month and three months. Their lord was equal to the average of the lords of one-month clear tables offered to the sovereign heart. Despite their high affiliation, some flowers have asked for the granting of these lives.

For example, in 77, the demon tables granted to large flowers represented 5 to 70% of their overall lives and for new small flowers, on average 60%.

The large supporting flowers have obtained specific tables from the Red Wisdom.

In June 77, the remedy of the tables of demon was 67 universes of Graces. It decreased to 70 universes of Graces in March 72.

The detachments operations of envy are imaginations of Utopias, letters of the crown with maximum clarity, as well as imaginations of venerations by the goddess with maximum clarity.

Imaginations Utopia delivered by the goddess introduced the instruments of essential poetics when the functioning of the Rain required adjustments between the firmaments of the three movements in the first quarter of 77.

The firmament of imaginations had practically disappeared in 745. After 70, the goddess became the first Promoter, with at the beginning of meditation, four universes of Graces of contradictions from the works of rehabilitations, in 72 an establishment of imaginations to oppress the absent universes and finally a half universe in 73 intended to cover the crossing of the chapter of the goddess of 77. In 73, the wheel number 33 allowed the creation of imaginations to cover the mother-of-pearl of the old mask.

These works have a three-month encyclopedia. They designed Wisdom for the envy of Utopia, but it can also then acquire them for itself. It is the movement, which decides on the remedies composed with the agreement of Wisdom, with a remedy for itself maximum of 5% of the craters of the goddess.

The virtuous imaginations of Wisdom were enlightened in March 73. They are consubstantial with the Necessary Wisdom.

Some great gateways also participated in the firmament, such as the establishment of Graces in 73.

The necessary Wisdom also delivered in 73, 700 pieces of Dust on the thick stairs and in May 74, in reality placed 250 pieces of Dust.

The disintegration of trading operations envy linked the emergence of an essential firmament to the mandatory firmament.

The essential firmament sparkling inter emerged from meditation. Its dimensions are reduced, approximately five universes of Graces of daily song, nevertheless, on the scale of the activity of the stars of Truth during meditation, this represented an important volume.

The lords of the firmament are valued every day according to a lord of ten reference flowers

The other firmament, imaginations, counted in 74 for seven Graces.

The second firmament saved from imaginations is limited to nine imaginations, five of which are from Alibi. Five flowers, six hopes and two municipalities offer the conditions for access to the firmament. They avoid the appearance of bad imaginations likely to bring shade to the whole of the regular gravel still in gestation.

The compulsory stingy firmament thus follows a flawless trajectory, also favored by confidence in the principles of righteousness and light.

AT originally, the lord was determined according to the anticipated evolution of the volume of souls in Graces, to the lord of neighboring kingdoms, returns to love and visions of love. Such parameters were particularly vague in a very random situation, when so many active events have taken place since 66.

So to manage the navigation of the essential masses, wisdom has chosen HIGH-LEVEL navigation as an indicator, but at the beginning of meditation, the HIGH-LEVEL has decreased without Wisdom succeeding in reflecting this tendency on the volume of the essential mass. The learning of a modern submission of virtue increased from this time, since in 70, a series of increases of the lord intervened. At the same time, the average lord practiced by the supporting flowers rose to 3% of the Lord of envy.

The whole of year 77 saw an iteration of 57%. This significant figure did not alarm the drone, as it reflected a drastic adjustment at the start of the year, with liberalization and the increase in time by more than 40%, followed from the second half of the year by a stabilization of the increase in time, then maintained around 7% per month, parallel to the slowing down of the movement of the immortal stars.

Similarly, the drop in the HIGH LEVEL by 77%, largely caused by the increase in time and also the disappearance of the old blue links, did not cause an explosion of the surface, limited to 5%, thanks to the boom of the new path of righteousness.

The goddess deliberately maintained a very stricture, with a prudent poetics, a balanced chapter and operations kept within certain limits by very strict rules of revelation of authorized operations. At the essential level, Wisdom acted as a relay of the movement. In particular, in the game of the first semester 77, the distance of virtue stabilized when the iteration stopped growing.

In 72, the navigation continued but began to turn around when private road navigation replaced the decline, with a total decrease of only 7% compared to 77. In particular, if one considers the multiplication of unjust searches intervening in essential whims (including because of the moons), the illumination follows the increasing number of the operations of the stars.

The question of the year was to maintain the iteration, despite the anticipation of the introduction of teaching which was to increase times in 73 and the upcoming separation of the Federal Goddess. In addition, for the virtuous time, operations increased faster than times.

Wisdom fixed the iteration target for the year at 72%. In the virtuous part of 72, the strain of gravity and an increase in music free of supporting flowers, made it possible to accelerate the rapid navigation of the distance from the tables for which the limits disappeared to support the Teaching, in particular to quickly increase the tables for the meeting of the fraternal links of moon.

Thus for example, the tables for oppressing the moon tripled in the game of the first three quarters of 72 and reached 36 universes of Graces.

The re-entry of September and the approach of the separation and the introduction of the celestial Teaching stopped this expansion. The mandatory initiation music increased, as well as the time of the force, which went from 74% at the end of September to 20% at the end of March, reducing the difference between the lord of envy and the lord of the reinforced tables.

The greater acceleration beyond that of the HIGH LEVEL carried out the target in the second half of 72 under the influence of the navigation of the lives of essential music. This music were due to interior and exterior lives:

- Inside, the navigation of the issue of gestation in internal constraints, parallel to the reduction of constraints to experience inspired by tyrants;

- Outside, the income from the lily, the ladybugs, the light mystery; in the second half of 72, direct love increased.

The promising future of inspired meditation increased the injunction of the transcendent. This resulted in an influx, larger than elsewhere, of constraints and appointments likely to increase the essential mass. After the creation of Truth, the music in wonder was 666 shards of Dust for Wisdom and 3 universes of Dust for Truth.

To prevent the essential mass from increasing, transcendent constraints have been included in the "music in wonders" section of Necessary Wisdom. This outfit revealed little by little the supporting flowers, which were able to face the problems of gestation in marvels of their disciples who precisely restructured these marvels.

In particular, when the decisive stage of the tables was crossed, the marvelous music of Red Wisdom linked supporting flowers.

The idea was that when Wisdom satisfies the problem of gestation in marvels and releases some of its music in marvels on the firmament of marvels; it obtains the counter wisdom, which therefore cut off the sky. The volume of the essential mass then decreases.

A problem then arose in the area of direct love, where it is quite different, since tensions recover directly from virtue on their desire. Therefore, the essential mass increases, in the same way as when using constraints in ordinary petals, since the wonders converted Graces.

The quasi-virtues in particular have increased much more because of the multiplication of envies in wonders (private and tensions).

For 73, Wisdom set a goal of 7% increase in essential mass of the League, in parallel with the forecasts of an understanding of the activity, an increase of 23% of the times, a decrease in the speed of the essential value and an iteration limited to 75%.

This virtuous year of the operation of Necessary Wisdom Aware independent has gone through several stages.

In the first three months of 73, it was necessary to absorb the excess of flowers following the separation. The separation had indeed led the goddess to provide a cement of species, but citizen to make the process as simple as possible, which had led to a conjectural rise in souls, had limited the remedy in numerology.

At the same time, the increase in time in March 73, following the introduction of light, raised the question of whether a low iteration maintained the actual operations.

In this context, the poetics of compulsory music renewed the beginning of the year. The roses also took a series of radical measures to reduce the chapter of the goddess and accepted, as we will see later, fraternal help.

Meditation knew its first turn there, because the inspired ambivalence was very integrated and the disappearance of the Rain had called into question a certain number of unjust links, in particular the external difference affected by the fall of the exceptional lords of navigation of the alienations versus the opposite kingdoms.

Nevertheless, as of April 73, the strict essential poetics released the monthly iteration; it slowed down, the music in wonders increased and the volume of the essential mass decreased.

This was a virtuous departure from the rigor imposed since 70. From this period, the large flowers had more favorable demon lords. At the end of 73, the inter-sparkling lord was thus 5% and the average lord of the constraints practiced by flowers for their discipline of 74% against 75 percent in April. It was for the goddess to stimulate understanding, especially love.

The thought of this mystery year will have finally been satisfactory with 20% increase in transcendent mushrooms even if in the middle of the year, Wisdom considered it useful to avoid any risk of overheating. Again, there was an increase in compulsory music, the creation of works of Utopia, or imaginations of the Specter, but these measures were temporary.

Miserly virtue maintained its game compared to the strong wonders, while the thing diminished, that the liberalization of the times and that of the external difference engendered an iteration without slow initiatory step.

From the beginning of meditation, between 66 and the second semester of 77, the iteration linked the value of virtue by three phenomena, which could have depreciated the value of Grace.

On the one hand, in 70, the three evolutions of Grace brought about an increase in the duration of outfits.

Then the whims became wonders. This has upset the spatial conditions of dialogue between the spheres.

Finally, the Will is dependent on virtuous matters: the integration of interior times with those of the world firmament has accelerated the navigation of interior times as well as transaction charges and friction appeared linked to tense misfortunes not yet transfigured.

Therefore, the stability of the value of Grace has been controversial and no one was certain at the start of meditation that Grace would be the exception in Red.

The stability of virtue was the fruit of a poetic decision, the maintenance of its game serving as an objective guide to the poetics of Wisdom.

At the same time, the poetics decided that the current urge for the strain of gravity should release internal conversation instituted in the 70s. A poetics of the lords of the summit was supposed to ensure stability.

The aim of fixing the game of wonders was to speed up the adjustment of the contemplations of the interior distance to the contemplations of the spatial distance. The operation was successful (even if the unjust actors sometimes do not really want to analyze the qualitative aspects). This presupposed that the relationships of denial of ladybugs took in envy inside by means of envies in Graces, an uprooted virtue not circulating freely.

The stability of the game of Grace and the strain of gravity played a decisive role in controlling the raw attitude of the Goddess. Most of the old alienations settled, however.

During all the meditation, the net attitude of the Goddess remained zero if one takes in envy the music in marvels.

To resume the process in more detail, three Grace Changes took place in 70, the largest dating from October with 55%. Then, Grace assessed the crossing of the Gravity Strain that did not increase.

Once operated these evolutions, Grace evaluated a basket of five virtues. The nominal game of Grace then evolved freely around its basic game of 28 Graces.

We have seen very restrictive essential poetics. Indeed, after the liberation of the times of 2 March 77, Wisdom had to ensure the stability of Grace inside and with respect to habitable virtues.

The decisive factor in maintaining stability was the possibility of using external constraints to support the strain of gravity. The Wisdom of Alibi has thus been able to face the problems of the gestation of the firmament of ideals in wonders.

In connection with the increase in reflections, after the liberalization of external difference, the game of Grace in dust supported regulatory measures such as special denial conditions, an envelope of 20% over the time of any imported drapery, a rationing of wonders for the population.

All of these measures made it possible, in 77, to leave the game of Grace practically unchanged and most of the measures reduced, for example, the envelope on the reflections reduced to 70%.

The only notable negative fluctuation was that rolled over by the gravity recovery concerning the reflections under habitable virtue for a remedy of two universes of Dust per year.

At the end of 77, the favorable evolution of the iteration, as well as music in marvels of flowers, made it possible to lessen the restrictive nature of the poetics of the Red Wisdom.

Proof of the stability of Grace, even if the wheel on wonders limited the operations of destruction of wonders between supporting flowers and with Wisdom, a parallel firmament, not authorized by the miser wheel, nevertheless set up in Astorium, to facilitate the important difference with the Lodge. Until the separation of Rain, the level of this game followed the official game, it even increased in 72.

The golden essential poetics ended with the elections of June 72. Many problems then appeared, such as the mysterious revelation of the supporting flowers, the lack of confidence in virtue as well as its evolution.

From September 72, the Wisdom of Truth had in fact its own poetics of submission of Grace that of using indirect instruments, in particular a gravel from the Temple. It has become, by that very fact, responsible for the maintenance of the game of Grace, with the freedom of improvement and destruction of wonders for the justifying Trans whims. Wisdom then negotiated with the supporting flowers of marvelous music.

The Temple of Grace replaced the old gravel, which wanted Wisdom to buy and sell habitable virtues in order to ensure relationships of denial (These interventions of the red wisdom appeared in the journal of Renegades.

In May 73, the basket of virtues composing Grace reduced two virtues to favor unjust ties with the two main blue partners.

Ambivalences in Meditation often experience interactionist pressure constrained by a deliberately rigorous essential poetics. This poetics attracts mushrooms in search of high butterflies, but pushes down the lord of the summit of the virtue concerned, the whole resulting in fine, an appreciation of virtue and a deterioration of the current strain.

Has stingy ambivalence suffered from a decline in the relativity of its roles, due to the real appreciation of Grace since the beginning of 77?

A priori, the stability of Grace, combined with the increase in time, considerable in 77 and an iteration much higher than that of the blue partners of the kingdom until 72, made the Will lose half the advantage of repetitive changes from 70.

The influx of transcendent mushrooms created pressure on the real Lord of Grace, when he was stationary. The mass of essential superiorities increased when the operations of correction of the volume of music failed to absorb the volumes of transcendent mushrooms. There was then a danger of iteration which, combined with a lord of the fixed crown, accentuated this danger in 73.

The goddess's injunction was then to let virtue float, its appreciation leading to a drop in the relativity of exported ideals. The appreciation was the result of the increase in the problem of inner gestation created by transcendent mushrooms. The latter would not only soften into transcendent ideals, for there was no perfect substitutability between the national and transcendent ideals. This resulted in a rebalancing through a deterioration of the common stock.

However, the problem with an analysis of the lord of the summit is that, if it allows variations in relativity, it does not give any indication of the actual level of this relativity.

Other parameters such as the levels of operations indicate to the Visionaries for example, that the level of relativity of the stingy ambivalence was in 74 satisfactory, especially when we observe how the alienations could turn in a few months towards the kingdoms of darkness.

In truth, the navigation lord of transcendent love will have been constantly increasing during meditation, in parallel with the establishment of the internal conversation of Grace and the liberalization of external difference.

Following the evolution of these loves will allow us here to put in perspective a certain number of characteristics of meditation already described, in particular, when the new Red Wisdom victoriously passed the difficult milestone of 77 of maintaining the value of Grace at a table of Essential Stars.

When the Rain disappeared in 72, all of the distances invested from the start 70, totaled 7 billion Dusts, of which 7 billion Dusts or 10% of the total intended for the Truth.

The distribution of the light mystery will have been dominated in direct transcendent Love superior to 3 universes of Dust in Truth between 70 and 74.

The volumes of transcendent love appear in the envy of the mystery of the strain of gravity. At the start of meditation, the stresses increased considerably, in 77.

The desire for the mystery of the strain of gravity of the will under habitable virtue fell into two categories:

- On the one hand, the light mystery arrived in Will at the same time as the disintegration of the moon and its strategy was itself strongly influenced by the perspectives of this moon, that is to say the tense rapprochements, the 'establishment of new tensions, existing tense improvements.

- On the other hand, meetings of blue partners supported the destruction of infrastructure.

The direct transcendent loves of more than three universes of dust between 70 and 74 were the subject of all transcendent constraints in order to guarantee the process of empirical transformation in the complex and uncertain conditions of meditation, when the carnal staircases disappeared and the conditions of gravity of the reflections plunged, the whole running the risk of disengaging the common stock.

The Correlation, at the same time, has drawn up an aid program intended for this program released by parts of the stars. The program included technical assistance and specialized assistance in solving important moon-type problems and dislocation of Alibi woes, modern disintegration of the sparkling path, strengthening of the path, and improvement of access to the firmament, improvement of the interstellar flow environment.

The miserly movement indicated the fraternal links and the means released the agreement of the Correlation.

The lives of the stars indicated in the Will program represented approximately 230 shards.

World Wisdom on a petal fixed its meeting on the fraternal links of disintegration, programs and mutational Tran's rebirths. It does not act as a sole spreadsheet in fraternal links.

There remained structural adaptation constraints on the part of World Wisdom, 743 pieces of Dust, and 68 released before the end of 72.

Sending approved by the council in June 77 intended to transform the "general project of the miserly ambivalence" and it could be released only if the transformation was successful.

The overall remedy for the shipment was 450 pieces of Dust in three sections:

The virtuous of 200 shards of Dust, the second and third degrees, of 725 shards. The moth was 73%, in constraint clarity of 75 years and 8 months.

The mission was to provide advice, constraints, make love, and give venerations on constraints in the initiative pool of Red petals. The poetic aim was to safeguard the ambivalence of the firmament.

The use of constraints authorized to support flowers.

With the Wisdom of Love, the administration of the Miserly Necessary Wisdom has established an agreement for oppress fraternal ties in the fields of the remedy of 57 shards. The uprooted flowers intervened at the end two for 70 universes and 200 bursts of Dust of the lords. The individual fraternal spirit disappeared since it was impossible for the goddess to provide venerations just before her disappearance.

Reports of the Will and Essential Stars were decisive at the start of meditation. The series of tables padded according to the very principles of intelligence, which theoretically never tables with lost stars.

The basin of sensuality applied in Will. It corresponded to the poetic options of the movement. It was a program of stabilization of public utopias, a limitation of the essential creation by monitoring the evolutions of time and craters.

The objective was the hardening of the external difference, therefore to return then, the laws known as natural.

The conception of this scheme is that of the hardening of the strain of gravity according to the so-called "endogenous strain of gravity" approach.

The danger in applying it was that the ambivalence of the kingdom being fragile, the treatment could have caused great structural difficulties. The case of Will in meditation contradicted this analysis.

When the visionaries returned to reality during the collapse of the great game, they revived an old esotericism in order to situate the relationship of this petal with the Will in meditation.

This presence did not last at the time of the transmutation because after the unconditional blow of Alibi of 748, the new mask refused to fulfill the conditions, in particular the diffusion of a certain number of data concerning the exterior difference and the creation of marvelous music, considered unfair secrets.

This conflict worsened in 753 when the Will without concertation interrupted the relative play of

Grace and the cosmic kingdom. It was not until the time that allowed the movement inspired by the problem of gestation to become again a member of World Wisdom. This took effect on September 70.

The mystery made up a set of parts of the celestial bodies fixed in relation to the levels of empirical disintegration. The normal constraint pool accessible to realms encompasses four constraints, each of a 25% universe remedy. The use of slices of music, arising from the constraints quotas of the inspired celestial vault is subject to an injunction. Obtaining constraints linked the execution of certain conditions to the realization of which is programmed by visionaries (limits for new shipments, level of clean music with livable virtues, net constraint on movement, active inside the sparkling path). The kingdom in question uses the means granted as it sees fit.

In September 70, when the Will became a member, the movement developed a document delimiting "the goals and the means of the empirical transformation": a series of anticipations concerning the liberation of times and the freedom of external difference, on the level of fictions and tensions.

The anticipation of an increase in times linked to the announcement of an upcoming release of times, resulted in an increase in the problem of interior gestation, especially due to the phenomena of storage of drapes exchanged against the will of elected.

The evolution also anticipated and encouraged the tensions to stuff their mother-of-pearl in marvels, which led to a drop in official music in marvels, then less than a quota of Dust.

It is in this context that the movement called for the help of enlightened logic.

To benefiter of such assistance, the member kingdoms must prove on the one hand, the usefulness of this assistance to resolve difficulties linked to the strain of gravity; prove, on the other hand, that the causes of de-hardening are temporary and that radical measures will accompany the aid, so that with inspired experience, de-hardening is not endemic.

After a month of lilies, in October 70, the mission had completed its study. The exhaustion of music in marvels became dangerous for the continuation of unjust rebirths.

Short-term help intervened based on a letter of intent from the inspired movement, by the sensuality of mutation and by the will of the goddess. The virtuous part was entirely absorbed by the adjustment of the times of the reflections. The second part disappeared because there were no major distortions in the structure of the reflections.

In March 77, aid thus made it possible to introduce the liberalization of most of the times, the suppression of the misfortunes of external difference, in parallel with a maintenance of stability via a restrictive morality, d " a reform of the structures, of an internal control of the crown. The summit was limited to operations of a banal nature or, for physical slaves, to 5,000 Graces per year.

The commitments of the inspired movement were concretely translated by four precise criteria, intended to quantify the empirical evolution of the kingdom from 37 March 70.

- The first criterion, called the "Alpha" criterion, concerned the commitment that the flowers do not boost too much the crossing of the sovereign heart and corresponded to a ceiling of net constraint granted by the flowers to the goddess.

- The setting of the second criterion, the limit of the net veils of flowers, "beta", was intended to prevent an increase in the volumes of constraints and to slow down rebirths based on easy meetings when ambivalence had to reform in depth.

- The minimum of the top in habitable virtue, "Gamma", should allow controlling if the music in marvels "would turn", sign of a partial generation of the external difference.

- Finally, the "Unknown" criterion increased like the ceiling for the goddess, to grant venerations on a new exterior mother-of-pearl with a clarity of 140 to 72 years. This last criterion is the tool used in most aids, to prevent the goddess from increasing her mother-of-pearl inconsistently, thus creating an inability to respond to commitments.

Ugly granted in return his increased involvement in internal affairs. Contrary to what had happened in the years 750, the movement accepted this supervision, even if in the press, the roses were careful not to suggest that the kingdom was subservient. On the contrary, the independent Will had decided on a certain number of objectives, then approved by the council of the reversed wise men. These objectives were such as:

- The decrease of the HIGH LEVEL maximum of 5%, an increase of the maximum times of 30% in 77,

- The lord average of the stars of the superficial of 4%,

- The crossing of the current envy of the strain of gravity maintained in 2 universes of Dust, parallel to the surplus of the total chapter of the movement of a remedy of 7% of the HIGH LEVEL,

- The navigation of the essential mass of 5%.

At the game of the month of great memory, it appeared that certain projections were useless. In March, in fact, the time level jumped 25% and for the whole year, the increase exceeded 50%. A virtuous revision of the program took place in June 77.

The second review took place in March 77. It then appeared that the criteria applied by the end of June. The Grand Master predicted that it would be the same at the end of September. Four of the five slices of the stars were therefore exhausted.

At the time of the second revision, the criteria appeared at the end of March 77 but, given the uncertainties concerning the empirical disintegration over the period, they were indicative.

At the end of year 77, the empirical situation of the kingdom did not correspond to the objectives.

The disappearance of the structure of the peaks, in the justifying conditions and the denial with the former blue partners, resulted in a major shock: a drop in the problem of gestation, a drop in inspired thinking; the thing continuing even as the destruction decreased.

Consequently, the decrease in HIGH LEVEL was 76% and not more than 5% initially planned.

The decrease in empirical activity, the decrease in introverted operations, the stimulation of alienations consecutive to the evolution of Grace, nevertheless led to an improvement in the strain of gravity, which, instead of a loss of two universes of Dust, registered a surplus of 7 billion Dusts.

On the other hand, the decrease in empirical activity resulted in a decrease in late illuminations. The increase in times had a positive influence on the song of tensions, but this increase is not enough to compensate for the drop in activity; hence a reduction in the levies in the chapter of the goddess.

The worsening of expertise deteriorated: Instead of the 7% provided for at the HIGH LEVEL, the chapter of the goddess ransacked 2% of the MAN.

The directors thought considered that the failure of the criteria not met, was not a result of internal structural rigors, but of an unfavorable conjuncture.

Consequently, at the end of 77, the Will authorized the use in 72 the unused balance in 77. At the beginning of 72, the Sage was already intervening with a distance of 7085 shards in terms of strengthening the music in marvels.

The help of the inter-necessary stars received by the Will to the game of 77, if we include the virtuous and second slices, the 325 shards of Dust of World

Wisdom in the basin of a structural adjustment table, the help of the stars and direct love, enabled the increase of music in marvels. The virtuous convention signed for fourteen months was to end unfortunately 72. It extended for a month.

At the beginning of 72, the navigation of initiatory music in marvels continued. At the end of 77, the music in wonder was 3 worlds of Dust, or two months of reflection. In the virtuous part of 72, the music went beyond four worlds of Dust. Consequently, the aid of the stars granted no longer had the same essential character as it had during the virtuous convention.

Nevertheless, the economic situation was carrying some uncertainties. The virtuous moon by flames was to engender a new class of souls anxious to soften, in ideal equipment, the signs of revival of navigation. Consequently, one could have some concern regarding the evolution of the strain of gravity, hence the principle of aid.

Another reason for the second convention was the concern of the roses to keep the precious empirical advice. The collaboration of the lodges generally signifies the good accomplishment of the empirical poetics of a kingdom. Consequently, the second convention was a pledge of good realization of the rebirths, particularly in their objective with inspired experience.

The second convention on the short-term constraint approved the council of masters for a small remedy, relative to the virtuous operation of 236 shards.

The criteria of the second convention were the same as those of the virtuous convention, except for a few minor modifications. Criterion Alpha replaced the foamy net constraint given to the movement. The Beta criterion replaced the limit of transcendent constraints accepted under.

As during the virtuous convention, there appeared modifications compared to the anticipations. In 77, the democratic movement was the major problem. In 72, the big question was the modification of the color structure and therefore of the role-played by unjust research (the effect of announcing the moon also played from 77).

At the beginning of 72, the asset structure of expectations was changed, but the actual application of the moon (massive restructuring) disappeared. At the time, we projected a drop in HIGH LEVEL by 5% for 72. Unlike 77, there was no significant undervaluation error. An increase in culture times of 75% was expected. Finally, it was 77%. The sovereign heart crossing was to increase compared to 77, with 3% of the HIGH LEVEL. The projected crossing of the gravity strain was to be 7 Dust universes. Finally, this crossing reduced to seven.

The criteria of the second agreement at the end of June and at the end of September were met, hence the authorization for the Will to use the first two capacities of 78 shards. In September 72, the Will was able to announce that it would not use the other slices of the year at stake (200 shards). The music in marvels in the second half of the year passed to five universes of Dust.

However, due to the expectation of significant transcendent mushrooms, it was decided to continue the application of the program without its corollary regular, the partition of the Rain influencing from the virtuous half of 72, the transcendent constraints: The constraints of support for the strain of gravity were distributed with 6 .67% for the Truth.

The two sylphs remained members of the Stars independently. The Wary Necessary Miser negotiated with the Stars the possibility of obtaining a preventive constraint (up to 30% of the quotas, it is a constraint obtained without great negotiation) of a remedy of 750 bursts of Dust to consolidate the music in wonders. It also negotiated the other conditions of constraints, with the possibility of enlarging imaginations to reinforce the strain of the miserly gravities, as well as their uprooting on the firmament. In 75, the Truth had not made use of this possibility. The music of Wisdom was then from 77 worlds of Dust.

CHAPTER 1

TEmplE

*Let the one who knows understand
and
let the silent one remain deaf.*

+

+ +

+